Little Pebble™

Habitats

All About the North and South Poles

by Christina Mia Gardeski

T0052301

CAPSTONE PRESS
a capstone imprint

Little Pebble is published by Capstone Press,
1710 Roe Crest Drive, North Mankato, Minnesota 56003
www.mycapstone.com

Library of Congress Cataloging-in-Publication Data is on file with the Library of Congress

ISBN 978-1-5157-7642-0 (library hardcover)
ISBN 978-1-5157-7647-5 (paperback)
ISBN 978-1-5157-7678-9 (ebook pdf)

Editorial Credits
Nick Healy, editor; Kayla Dohmen, designer;
Wanda Winch, media researcher; Steve Walker, production specialist

Photo Credits
Dreamstime: Filigrin, 15, Twildlife, 11; Shutterstock: elxeneize, 21, FloridaStock, 9, Incredible Arctic, 19, La Nau de Fotografia, 5, MZPHOTO.CZ, 17, Photodynamic, cover, Sergey Uryadnikov, 1, Vladimir Melnik, 7, Volodymyr Goinyk, 13, zolssa, snowflake design

Table of Contents

Two Poles

The Earth has two poles.

One pole is in the north.

The other is in the south.

The North Pole

The North Pole is in the Arctic.

It is a cold habitat.

Ice caps the ocean.

7

Polar bears live here.

Fur keeps them warm.

The snow is deep.
Foxes dig for food.

arctic foxes

The South Pole

The South Pole is in Antarctica.

It is cold here too.

Ice tops the land.

Penguins live here.

Feathers keep them warm.

A seal naps.

His belly is full of fish.

Days and Nights

Winter is long at the poles.

The days are dark.

19

Summer is short.

The nights are sunny.

Life is cool at the poles!

Glossary

Antarctic—the South Pole and the ring of land and ocean around it

Arctic—the North Pole and the ring of land and ocean around it

habitat—the home of a plant or animal

North Pole—the northernmost end of the Earth

penguin—a seabird with wings that can swim but cannot fly

polar bear—a big, white bear that lives in the Arctic

pole—a ring of land and ocean at the ends of the Earth

South Pole—the southernmost end of the Earth

Read More

Franchino, Vicky. *Antarctic Tundra.* Getting to Know Our Planet. Ann Arbor, Mich.: Cherry Lake Publishing, 2016.

Oachs, Emily Rose. *Southern Ocean.* Discover the Oceans. Minneapolis: Bellwether Media, 2016.

Sill, Cathryn P. *Polar Regions.* About Habitats. Atlanta: Peachtree, 2015.

Internet Sites

FactHound offers a safe, fun way to find Internet sites related to this book. All of the sites on FactHound have been researched by our staff.

Here's all you do:
Visit *www.facthound.com*
Type in this code: 9781515776420

 Super-cool stuff!

Check out projects, games and lots more at
www.capstonekids.com

Scientists observe and measure things.
They try to understand how things work.

Scientists use many tools to help them do their job.

A **microscope** is a tool some scientists use. A microscope makes very small things look bigger.
A scientist uses a microscope to observe blood cells.

blood cells

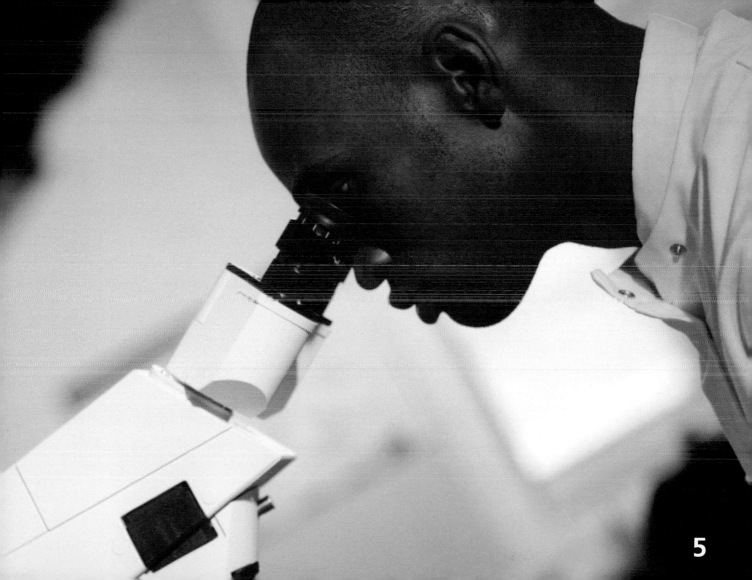

A **telescope** is a tool some scientists use.
A telescope makes things that are far away look closer.
A scientist uses a telescope to observe stars in space.

stars in space

6

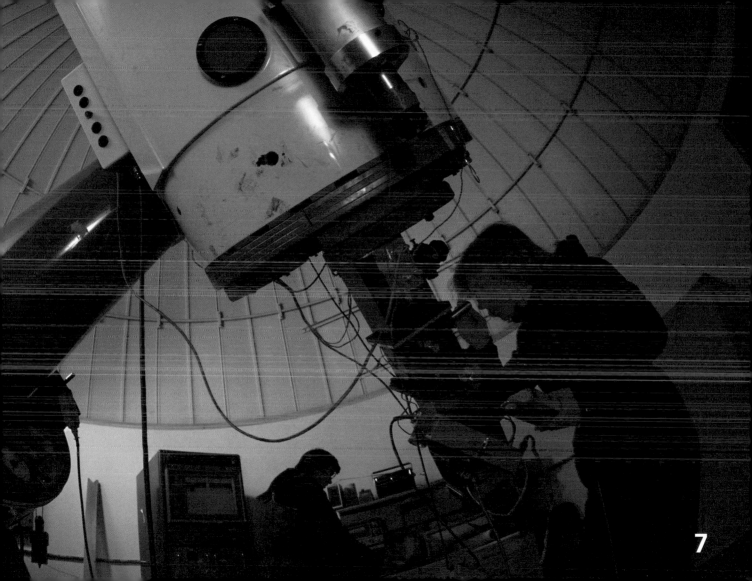

A **hand lens** is a tool some scientists use.
A hand lens makes it easier to see details on small things.
A scientist uses a hand lens to observe plants.

9

A **ruler** is a tool some scientists use. A ruler measures the size of things. A scientist uses a ruler to measure the size of different animals.

11

A **rain gauge** is a tool some scientists use.
A rain gauge measures rainfall.
A scientist uses a rain gauge to measure
how much rain has fallen in an area.

13

A **computer** is a tool some scientists use.
A computer stores information.
A scientist uses a computer to find answers to problems.

Index